The Father's Comfort

Published by Mark Gyde
First Published in Great Britain in 2019.
Copyright © Mark Gyde

British Library Cataloguing in Publication Data
ISBN: 978-1-7074938-8-3

The Father's Comfort

The Father's Comfort

Introduction

Comfort is a huge topic throughout the Bible. In one form or another, it is mentioned over 100 times and therefore it must be very important for us to understand. In fact, I would rather not refer to comfort as a 'topic' as that implies it is something that we have to understand or grasp with our mind. Comfort is not a topic in that sense, it is an experience. It is a powerful emotion that brings healing to the deepest wounds in our heart.

Before we look at this vast subject from a Biblical point of view, let's look at the dictionary definition as this sheds a lot of light on what comfort actually is:

Comfort: to bring relief from pain, distress or affliction, to satisfy, to strengthen within. To provide a sense of wellbeing. Quiet enjoyment.

This shows us very clearly that comfort is not a topic we grasp with our mind but is an emotion we experience, and as we do it brings relief to the turmoil and brokenness we feel in the depth of our heart. Comfort calms us, restores us and brings us to a place of contentment; it is the catalyst for bringing our heart to a place of peace. 'Comfortable' is perhaps another word we could use as it is more readily understood. We like to be comfortable in our home, with friends or in church; it describes a sense of wellbeing where we can start to relax and let the internal walls of our heart come down.

Despite being mentioned so frequently throughout the Bible, comfort is something that we don't talk about very often. As I travel in many different countries, I often ask how many times people have heard comfort being spoken about. I discover it is not something we talk about let alone something we allow ourselves to receive. All too often, the people I'm talking to have never heard anyone talk about comfort and this is a sad reflection of the orphan-hearted ways much of the church has settled for. Rather than being a comforting people we beat ourselves into more activity, putting to one side the affairs of the heart.

The more I look at comfort the more I see how immense it is. I am convinced it is something we continually need to receive in order that we can live out of the overflow of comfort. It should not be something we only seek when we need relief from our pain, distress or affliction.

Biblically I see comfort as an expression of love which goes to the core of our pain and brings us healing and wholeness.

Over the next few pages I'm going to look at how we can receive comfort, how we can live in it and how we can minister comfort to others.

Comfortless

Before we start to look at comfort let's take a few moments to look at what it means to comfortless, or un-comforted.

"Again, I observed all the oppression that takes place under the sun. I saw the tears of the oppressed, with no one to comfort them. The oppressors have great power, and there was no-one to comfort them. So I concluded that the dead are better off than the living. But most fortunate of all are those who are not yet born. For they have not seen all the evil that is done under the sun." (Ecclesiastes 4:1-3 NLT)

Solomon writes these words as he looks back over his long life which has had many ups and downs. His conclusion (in summary) is that a life without God is meaningless, and conversely a fruitful life comes out of a life-giving relationship with our Creator.

He sees people who have not been comforted and, what's more, they have no-one who is able to comfort them. He sees people who are oppressed and suffering under a great burden and he describes this as being too overwhelming and painful to bear. His conclusion is stark. We are better off dead rather than living without comfort. That is a bold statement but one we should take to heart as it shows the importance of receiving and living in comfort. Solomon, knowing comfort's importance, does not stop there. Those that have died had experienced a comfortless life. They knew what it was like to never know the satisfaction or inner strength that comes as our afflictions are relieved. Solomon's conclusion is it's better not to be born at all rather than to live uncomforted.

To me, this is a tragedy as it means living in a state of brokenness and despair with a yearning in our heart that is never satisfied. It means we live as we were never intended to. Rather than living in love, we live in despair which leads to hopelessness. When we are uncomforted we have to live with all the trauma that has accumulated in our heart.

Of course, we don't like to be comfortless and so we seek other things to fill the void. Maybe they relieve the pain for a season but many of these things can be false comforts. They are like medicine which only has a short-term effect; when the medicine has run its course the pain returns. The only thing that satisfies us permanently is the unconditional, comforting love of the Father.

Jesus is very concerned that we should not live without comfort. In John 14 he promises 'another Comforter' who will be with us forever (John 14:16). This Comforter is the Holy Spirit who lives in our heart and constantly reminds us that we are no longer orphans but are now children of God (John 1:12). This Comforter is the one who pours the Father's love into our heart and gives us the spirit of sonship which enables us cry 'Abba, Father'.

Comfort and Trauma

We all experience trauma and we experience it differently. What may be traumatic for one person may be inconsequential for another.

We all react to trauma differently. We may try and cope, maybe we try and fight our way through it, or perhaps we even pretend it has never happened. Ultimately the only solution to the trauma we've experienced is for us to receive comfort.

Trauma leaves us feeling emotionally empty and when we feel this way we need comfort. When we are in shock we need comfort. When we feel alone, abandoned, in pain, sick, wounded, broken, bereaved or rejected we need to experience comfort. Whatever the impact and effect that trauma has had on us, we need to experience a measure of comfort that surpasses and goes beyond the pain or wound we have experienced. Every trauma, however big or small has to be met with a greater level of comfort. To bring healing and wholeness, the comfort we need has to be greater than the source of pain. If not, we are left in pain or discomfort.

I see our heart as a container. In this container is trauma. It may have been there for so many years that we have accepted it's place in our heart. When we receive comfort it is like a liquid that goes down the inside edge of the container and settles underneath the trauma. As we go on receiving more comfort, the trauma begins to float on the measure of comfort we have received. But that is not enough. We need to receive more comfort than the trauma we have experienced in order that it can be lifted right out of our heart. Comfort goes under the trauma and forces it out leaving us with a comforted heart.

If we do not receive more comfort than the trauma we have received then we are left in pain and distress. We are left comfortless or in discomfort.

It is hard to quantify something so real as trauma. In which case how do we know how much comfort we need to receive? We go on receiving comfort until we know we are comforted and until that trauma ceases to have a hold on us. Instead of pain or distress we begin to feel comfortable.

It is not easy to face the trauma that may have settled in your heart. It can be painful. The good news is that you don't have to 'deal' with it yourself. It is giving Father permission to pour his comforting love into your heart in order that the trauma can float away. To see trauma go we have to identify the point of pain, or as a friend of mine says we have to go to the 'ouch' moment. What was the point of pain which caused that trauma to settle in your heart? Then, and this can be the hard bit, we need to stay in the 'ouch' moment so Father can comfort us. I encourage you stay in that place until you know you are comforted. This is not a quick process, it can take years for us to be truly comforted. Go on receiving comfort for you **will** be comforted.

"Comfort, comfort my people,
says your God.

Speak tenderly to Jerusalem,
and proclaim to her
that her hard service has been completed,
that her sin has been paid for,
that she has received from the Lord's hand
double for all her sins." (Isaiah 40:1-2)

When Isaiah says 'comfort, comfort' what he is really saying is that we are 'greatly comforted'. Our Father wants to greatly comfort us in all our troubles. The comfort we receive comes from the Father with tenderness, gentleness and compassion.

"For the Lord comforts Zion;
he comforts all her waste places
and makes her wilderness like Eden,
her desert like the garden of the Lord;
joy and gladness will be found in her,
thanksgiving and the voice of song." (Isaiah 51:3 ESV)

As we are comforted for all the trauma we have experienced the barren and empty places of our heart will be transformed. The desert of our heart is turned into a beautiful garden which is full of life. Instead of the sadness and sorrow which comes from a broken heart we begin to encounter joy and gladness. Our heart comes alive and is filled with a song of thanksgiving.

We become free.

Comfort When We Mourn

"Blessed are those who mourn, for they shall be comforted." (Matthew 5:4)

"The Spirit of the Sovereign Lord is on me,
because the Lord has anointed me
to proclaim good news to the poor.
He has sent me to bind up the broken hearted,
to proclaim freedom for the captives
and release from darkness for the prisoners,
to proclaim the year of the Lord's favour
and the day of vengeance of our God,
to comfort all who mourn,
and provide for those who grieve in Zion—
to bestow on them a crown of beauty
instead of ashes,
the oil of joy
instead of mourning,
and a garment of praise
instead of a spirit of despair." (Isaiah 61:1-3)

We can lose our job, our possessions, our home, our income, our friends, our pets, our church or even the painful loss of a loved one. There will be times of loss for all of us. Loss often comes unannounced, it is always significant and can affect us deeply.

When we suffer loss we need to be able to mourn our loss as it is part of the natural grieving process. Some may mourn in private, but it is only a hard heart that faces loss without going through a subsequent grieving process. In fact, I'm not sure we actually do face the loss unless we go through a season of mourning. Mourning is, I believe, a God-given gift which enables us to be healed and for our heart to be cleansed. Without it the pain is buried in our heart. It festers and produces only bitterness and resentment.

Mourning allows us to release that which we've lost and in time begin to be renewed.

When we mourn we are comforted. I particularly like how The Message translates the beatitude I mentioned above:

"You're blessed when you feel you've lost what is most dear to you. Only then can you be embraced by the One most dear to you."

When we mourn, we allow ourselves to be embraced and held in perfect love. We are held in the Father's arms in the same way as a shepherd carries a lamb (Isaiah 40:11) and we are comforted. We are nurtured in a way that strengthens and heals us. Isaiah describes this as an aspect of the Father's mothering love for us:

"As a mother comforts her child, so will I comfort you; and you will be comforted over Jerusalem." (Isaiah 66:13)

Mourning is not just about the big losses in our life, it is something we need to do for every loss. Are we sensitive to our own heart and able to discern the loss? If so, we can then allow ourselves to mourn. As we do, we bring our heart to the Father so we can receive more of his love and to experience him loving us. If our heart is dull to the loss we have experienced then it becomes hard and maybe even closed.

Love always creates an open heart and an open heart is one that is being healed and restored.

Just as we are sensitive to our own heart so we become sensitive to the hearts of others. We recognise their loss as being important to them. Even if it is not something that would affect us, for them it is significant. When they suffer loss we are able to comfort them. We can give them time and space to grieve their loss and can encourage them to receive the Father's comfort.

We all mourn in different ways and it can take varying lengths of time. But mourning is an important and necessary way of coming to terms with loss. Allowing ourselves to be comforted through that process enables our heart to be healed and restored.

Forgiveness and Repentance

The Psalms, in particular, are a celebration of the Father's forgiveness and the mercy and grace we receive from him.

"The Lord is gracious and compassionate, slow to anger and rich in love. The Lord is good to all; he has compassion on all he has made." (Psalm 145:8-9)

"But with you there is forgiveness, so that we can, with reverence, serve you.
Israel, put your hope in the Lord,
for with the Lord is unfailing love
and with him is full redemption.
He himself will redeem Israel
from all their sins." (Psalm 130:4,7-8)

King David made a big mistake. He committed murder in order that he could commit adultery and then he tried to cover it up. Nathan, the prophet, saw right through it as he told that beautifully simple story of the poor man with a single lamb (2 Samuel 12:1-8). David, as king, could have reacted with anger and had Nathan killed or imprisoned, but instead that story brought him to repentance.

We read of that repentance in Psalm 51 where David acknowledges his sin and asks for forgiveness. His heart, rather than being hard and closed, is open and he cries out for a renewed heart that is clean and pure. This cry is not only one of repentance, but also a recognition of the need David had to be comforted. His repentance became the way for him to be comforted.

"Create in me a pure heart, O God, and renew a steadfast spirit within me. Do not cast me from your presence or take your Holy Spirit from me. Restore to me the joy of your salvation and grant me a willing spirit, to sustain me." (Psalm 51:10-12)

We don't know everything about King David's past, but we do know that he was able to live out of the overflow of comfort, much of which may have come from his encounter with Nathan. In Psalm 131 David gives us a beautiful picture of extreme comfort and satisfaction:

"My heart is not proud, Lord,
my eyes are not haughty;
I do not concern myself with great matters
or things too wonderful for me.
But I have calmed and quieted myself,
I am like a weaned child with its mother;
like a weaned child I am content.
Israel, put your hope in the Lord
both now and forevermore." (Psalm 131)

Like David, as we repent and turn back to Father we open our heart to receive his comfort. Repentance means turning right round and walking in the opposite direction, it is a complete change of heart. Our repentance leads to our salvation and it is a significant factor for our heart as it finds the rest and peace it seeks after.

"In repentance and rest is your salvation, in quietness and trust is your strength, but you would have none of it." (Isaiah 30:15)

His love will always comfort and the more we lean into it the more we will receive.

"May your unfailing love be my comfort, according to your promise to your servant." (Psalm 119:76)

As we turn to him in repentance, we are comforted and we receive his forgiveness. Civil authorities require there to be a punishment when a wrong is committed and in society that is necessary in order to uphold the rule of law. However, in the Kingdom we are recipients of grace and mercy. When Jesus highlighted sin in people's lives he did not judge or condemn, but rather said 'go and sin no more'. I'm sure he looked at them with eyes of compassion and the love they received from that look was enough to transform their life.

Jesus wanted people to be free and the words he spoke gave people that freedom. As they encountered him they would have encountered the unconditional love of the Father which can't help but comfort.

Paul exhorts us to have the same attitude in our dealings with other people.

"If anyone has caused grief, he has not so much grieved me as he has grieved all of you to some extent—not to put it too severely. The punishment inflicted on him by the majority is sufficient. Now instead, you ought to

forgive and comfort him, so that he will not be overwhelmed by excessive sorrow. I urge you, therefore, to reaffirm your love for him." (2 Corinthians 2:5-8)

It is punishment enough for our brothers or sisters to know that they have wronged and hurt us. There is no further judgment or punishment necessary. Instead we should embrace them with love, forgiving and comforting them, so that they may be restored back into relationship and allow their heart to be healed.

In too many cases we play the role of jury and judge (at least so far as other people are concerned) when all we are called to do is love. Love is far more powerful than judgement and will have a much greater impact on other people's lives. As we forgive, we set people free in the same way that we are free through the forgiveness we ourselves have received.

Forgiveness is powerful, but it can be more powerful when combined with the comforting love of the Father. Just as we are comforted as we come in repentance and receive forgiveness so too we can forgive and comfort our brothers and sisters. As we do, it releases them to live from a free heart. Forgiveness restores relationship.

Another Comforter

The gospel stories don't mention the word comfort; however, we see it implicitly through the life of Jesus. He only did and said what he saw his Father doing and saying, he was the exact representation of his Father and so he most have been the most comforting person who ever lived. He was the person of love who made himself known to us.

We only have to think of the disparate group of men he called his disciples. A Zealot (someone who hated the Romans) being on the same team as a Roman tax collector. Two people, from totally different backgrounds, who would ordinarily hate each other are moulded together to form part of the early church. Peter said things as he saw them: bluntly! James and John, the sons of thunder. Martha's attitude when Mary left her to work alone in the kitchen. Jesus addressing sin in people's lives. All of these people encountered love and, I'm sure, comfort.

When Jesus fed the 5,000 he was concerned for their physical welfare. He didn't just perform an administrative miracle when he fed them, he comforted them. When Jesus calms the storm as the disciples are trying to row across the lake he simply says 'peace be still'; how comforting those words must have been.

Even when he is arrested and a disciple attacks one of the High Priest's servants, Jesus heals him and speaks comforting words 'no more of this'.

Interestingly, when Jesus was rejected at Nazareth (Luke 4:16-30) he moved to Capernaum and made it his home town. Capernaum means the village of comfort!

Jesus was a comforter.

In John 14, as Jesus prepares the disciples for his return to his Father he promises another Comforter, the Holy Spirit. In saying 'I will not leave you as orphans, I will come to you' (John 14:18) Jesus promises not to abandon them and he reassures them that the Holy Spirit will continue the work which he has begun. Through the Holy Spirit, Jesus and the Father promise to make their home in our heart (John 14:23).

The outpouring of comfort continues through the Holy Spirit, who pours the Father's love into our heart and enables us to cry 'Abba, Father'. The spirit of sonship, which is described for us in both Romans 8 and Galatians 4 enables us to live in comfort. It sets our heart free to live and walk as Jesus walked.

Comfort establishes us in sonship. It is a hallmark of Jesus' life and will become one for us as we are rooted and established in love.

"Now may our Lord Jesus Christ himself, and God our Father, who loved us and gave us eternal comfort and good hope through grace, comfort your hearts and establish them in every good work and word."
(2 Thessalonians 2:16-17 ESV)

We have not been left on our alone, nor are we required to work it all out for ourselves. We have another Comforter living in our heart who will cause us to walk in Father's ways.

The Father of ALL comfort

"Praise be to the God and Father of our Lord Jesus Christ, the Father of compassion and the God of all comfort, who comforts us in all our troubles, so that we can comfort those in any trouble with the comfort we ourselves receive from God. For just as we share abundantly in the sufferings of Christ, so also our comfort is abundant through Christ. If we are distressed, it is for your comfort and salvation; if we are comforted, it is for your comfort, which produces in you patient endurance of the same sufferings we suffer. And our hope for you is firm, because we know that just as you share in our sufferings, so also you share in our comfort." (2 Corinthians 1:3-7)

I hope that as you've read the previous pages you have begun to see how important it is for us to be comforted. I trust there is a longing in your heart to receive and experience this expression of love. If not a longing, then maybe a whisper or an awakening within you for something you know you need but have never been able to grasp.

If so, I urge you to pursue this with your whole heart. It is the Father's desire to pour his comforting love into your heart and it is something he does freely for all of us, no matter who we are or what our history is. This is not something he rations or hands out as a reward, but it is the fulfilment of his nature being birthed in us.

It is a free gift.

Comfort is also like the manna which was given to the Israelites on a daily basis as they wandered through the desert for forty years.

"Then the Lord said to Moses, "I will rain down bread from heaven for you. The people are to go out each day and gather enough for that day. In this way I will test them and see whether they will follow my instructions." (Exodus 16:4)

Every day without fail (except for the Sabbath when they received a double portion on the day before) there was new manna. However, the thing about the manna was that it landed on the ground outside their tents. It did not do them any good to sit in the tent doorway and look at the manna on the ground and say how wonderful it was. They had to get up, go outside and gather it in.

There was daily provision but they needed to do something in order to make it their own. It was not a question of them doing any work for they had received the abundant and free provision from their Heavenly Father. They had to gather it in. In other words, they had to receive the gift which had been freely given to them.

The comfort the Father pours into our heart is a daily provision and, as we shall shortly see, it is not just meant to comfort past hurts or trauma. It is given in order that we can build up a reservoir of comfort in our lives which will enable us to live from a free heart. Each and every day, we are recipients of the mercy and grace which flows freely from our Father's heart.

"The steadfast love of the Lord never ceases; his mercies never come to an end; they are new every morning; great is your faithfulness. 'The Lord is my portion,' says my soul, 'therefore I will hope in him'." (Lamentations 3:22-24 ESV)

We truly can rely on his love for us.

In John's first letter he encourages us to 'know and rely' on the love that God has for us (1 John 4:16). These are experiential words that change our heart; we know the love of God because we have experienced it and have become aware of the affect it has had, and is having, on our lives. John is describing a relationship rather than advising us to acquire knowledge about something. Filling our minds with the knowledge of God's love will not lead to us living in love, or as Paul puts it 'being rooted and grounded in love'.

The Father's love is not something that is turned on and off. It is not dependent on our behaviour but is a free flowing constant supply of love being poured into our heart by the Holy Spirit. But like the manna given to the Israelites it is a gift for us to receive. It is given, but we need to open our heart in order to receive it. There is a daily supply of comfort for us and all we need is an open and willing heart to receive.

As we read the book of Acts we see the physical hardship Paul endured as he went on his travels. Not only did he suffer being shipwrecked three times and a lot of danger as he travelled but he was beaten, whipped, imprisoned, stoned and left for dead. This was extreme suffering and Paul was obviously a tough man to survive all of this.

As we start to read 2 Corinthians we don't read about Paul's judgement or condemnation of his abusers. We don't see him seeking revenge or trying to promote himself.

Instead we read about comfort.

Through all his hardship and suffering Paul allows himself to be comforted. He comes to the God of **ALL** comfort, knowing he can be comforted for everything he has been through. I imagine that Paul lived being constantly comforted. He did not only seek it after times of trial or trauma, but he went into each day with a full reservoir of comfort in his heart. He lived in the source of comfort as he had discovered the reality of what Jesus talks about in John 14. Jesus says that he is in the Father, the Father is in him, we are in them and they are in us. Paul lived in the reality of being 'in Christ'.

So far as the Father is concerned we have *'joint seating with Christ in the Heavenly places'* (Ephesians 2:6 AMP), we are in him where he is. **We belong.**

As our heart finds its true home, we discover that being 'in Christ' means being held in love.

God is love, and so we begin to live in and experience perfect love in all its various expressions. This is why Paul knew God as the Father of all comfort. He lived it, breathed it and knew he had come home.

We see another glimpse of Paul's comforted heart at the end of this pastoral letter. In 2 Corinthians 11 and 12 Paul compares himself to the 'super-apostles' who are boasting in their own strength and who are seeking to take the people back into a life based on the law and observance of religious duty. Paul does not join them but rather boasts of his weakness and reliance on God, who we now know as the Father of all comfort. He has found the secret of contentedness. It is not relying on your own strength or abilities, but is the discovery and recognition of your own weakness which will lead you to be totally dependent on God. This discovery is the doorway to his power being released. It is the doorway to freedom.

A comforted heart does not need to self-promote but can take the path of apparent weakness. A comforted heart knows the secret of total reliance and dependency on the perfect Father. A comforted heart is at peace and can live in rest as it has come to know the Father (Matthew 11:25-30). A comforted heart can share that comfort with others. As we have been comforted so we can comfort others, not just with our own empathy, but with the very comfort we ourselves have received.

Our Father is the God of ALL comfort and this is a gift we can freely receive each and every day. I encourage you to gather this daily manna into your heart.

We have looked backwards at how we need to be comforted for the trauma we may have received over many years. We have seen how comfort brings healing to our broken heart and how it sets us free from the pain and woundedness of the past. We have seen how comfort is the fruit of our repentance and forgiveness. And we have seen how the abundant provision of comfort is like daily manna for us to gather into the storehouse of our heart.

Now we need to look forward.

Our Homecoming

In looking forward we need to recognise that comfort was never purely meant to be a sticking plaster for past hurts. It is possible for us to build a surplus of comfort in our heart which will enable us to live from a free heart. Instead of always playing 'catch-up' we will have the reserves and resources to live more fully from the heart, and therefore be living in a greater expression of freedom.

Too often we worry about our 'destiny'. What have we been called to do or to achieve? The problem is, in order to try and attain this destiny we end up with a lot of stress, self-righteousness or self-effort. It was never meant to be like this. I would rather we thought about our inheritance, as that is not something we strive towards. It is a gift that is ours simply because we are God's children. Our inheritance has already been won for us, everything that was needed to be done was done by Jesus on the cross. The gift has been given, there is no longer anything we have to earn.

In its simplest form our inheritance is to be sons and daughters, it is having a free heart, it is belonging to the Father's family and it is being continually being filled with the Spirit of Life. Our inheritance is to be at peace and in rest. None of my children had to do anything in order to become part of our family. They belong because they were born into it. We, too, are born (again) into the Father's family and then we belong. There is nothing more we need to do.

Living a comfort-filled life will enable us to live in the fullness of this inheritance. It will release us to become partakers of the glorious freedom of the sons of God. We will find that our lives are built on solid rock rather than on shifting sand and with such a foundation our lives will be enriched. In turn, we will enrich the lives of those around us. Living in love changes us and also changes the people we meet.

The latter part of the book of Isaiah paints a big picture which shows the Father's comfort. It is prophetically written and so the story applies as much to us as it did to Isaiah's original listeners.

I am merely selecting a few chapters to look at, but I encourage you to read chapters 40 to 66 so you can see the big picture for yourself.

Let me start in chapter 40:

"Comfort, comfort my people,
says your God.
Speak tenderly to Jerusalem,
and proclaim to her
that her hard service has been completed,
that her sin has been paid for,
that she has received from the Lord's hand
double for all her sins." (Isaiah 40:1-2)

We are greatly comforted as I have already mentioned. As we read on, we see that following the comforting of God's people, there is a revelation of his glory which we can interpret as a revelation of his nature and his personality.

"And the glory of the Lord will be revealed,
and all people will see it together.
For the mouth of the Lord has spoken." (Isaiah 40:5)

When Moses asked to see God's glory he too had a revelation of the personality and nature of God: loving, compassionate, slow to anger, faithful etc (Exodus 34:1-9).

A promise of Jesus is that he would pass on to us the glory that he has received from the Father. The Father's nature is to be revealed within us as we begin to walk as Jesus walked. A comforted heart will begin to reveal the glory of God. We will show off the nature and personality of the One living in us.

As his nature is revealed in us, we also experience a renewal and restoration of our soul. Verses 27-31 of chapter 40 describe for us the life and energy which we soak up when we abide in him. Please note, this life comes from him, it is not self-made or from our own resources. We live in his life; this is part of our inheritance.

The second chapter in Isaiah I want to look at is chapter 51.

Firstly, we are reminded where we come from. We are Abraham's children and also, as Paul reminds us in Galatians 3 and 4, the heirs of all the promises given to him. Abraham was to be a blessing to the nations of the world and that is what is also passed onto us. As the spirit of sonship lives in us we will become a blessing to the nations.

Once more we are reminded of the importance of comfort in this journey (v3 - ESV).

"For the Lord comforts Zion;
he comforts all her waste places
and makes her wilderness like Eden,
her desert like the garden of the Lord;
joy and gladness will be found in her,
thanksgiving and the voice of song."

We see that comfort leads to joy and gladness as the desert places of our heart are transformed into a beautiful garden. What a picture of redemption through comfort.

However, what I particularly want to draw out of this chapter is the treasure contained in verse 11.

"Those the Lord has rescued will return.
They will enter Zion with singing;
everlasting joy will crown their heads.
Gladness and joy will overtake them,
and sorrow and sighing will flee away." (Isaiah 51:11)

Comfort rescues us and brings our heart home. We see this no more clearly than in the story of the lost son in Luke 15. The welcoming embrace from the father stopped the son in his tracks. He has no opportunity to complete his prepared speech about only being a servant, he is fully welcomed back into the father's household and family.

How important it is for us to understand this with our heart. When the Father comforts us he brings us home. All the searching and striving can fall away. All the loneliness is taken away. We are home. We belong. We have found the place of contentment that all too often alludes us.

Whatever our history or our journey so far, we need a homecoming. I don't believe this is a one-off event but something we experience at a deeper level as we are drawn into the ocean of the Father's love. *(I have written more about this in my book 'The Depth of Love' – available on Amazon/Kindle).* There may be times Father says to you "you need a deeper homecoming". When he does, allow that part of your heart to come home. Our homecoming is part of our inheritance.

Let's turn back to Isaiah 35 where once again we see our homecoming as the result of being comforted.

"The desert and the parched land will be glad;
the wilderness will rejoice and blossom.
Like the crocus, it will burst into bloom;
it will rejoice greatly and shout for joy.
The glory of Lebanon will be given to it,
the splendour of Carmel and Sharon;
they will see the glory of the Lord,
the splendour of our God.

Strengthen the feeble hands,
steady the knees that give way;
say to those with fearful hearts,
'Be strong, do not fear;'" (Isaiah 35:1-4)

This is a very comforting passage. Fruitfulness will replace our former barrenness, the glory of the Lord will be revealed and fear will be driven away. Fear is the opposite of love and has no place in a heart which is dwelling in love, for perfect love casts out all fear (1 John 4:18).

Once again we see that renewal follows comfort.

"Then will the eyes of the blind be opened
and the ears of the deaf unstopped.
Then will the lame leap like a deer,
and the mute tongue shout for joy.
Water will gush forth in the wilderness
and streams in the desert.
The burning sand will become a pool,
the thirsty ground bubbling springs.
In the haunts where jackals once lay,
grass and reeds and papyrus will grow." (Isaiah 35:5-7)

And then we have our homecoming.

"And a highway will be there;
it will be called the Way of Holiness;
it will be for those who walk on that Way.
The unclean will not journey on it;
wicked fools will not go about on it.
No lion will be there,

nor any ravenous beast;
they will not be found there.
But only the redeemed will walk there,
and those the Lord has rescued will return.
They will enter Zion with singing;
everlasting joy will crown their heads.
Gladness and joy will overtake them,
and sorrow and sighing will flee away." (Isaiah 35:8-10)

Comfort and renewal will bring our heart home. This is the fullness of life which is our inheritance. We are not meant to be losers, always in need of a visit to the spiritual accident and emergency department. We are sons and daughters who have been set free to enjoy this life to the full (John 10:10).

The journey home is one of holiness. We are often put off by this word as it appears to be so unattainable. How can we possibly be holy? What do we have to do to be holy? How holy are we? These are all the wrong questions as holiness is not a substance which can be quantified. We are already holy through the sacrificial and redeeming work of Jesus. We certainly can't make ourselves more holy through our own effort. A comforted heart will be led into holiness because holiness describes the relationship we have with our Father. We cannot be truly holy without having been comforted, as it is the work of comfort which removes shame and guilt from our life.

Our homecoming is not to scoop us out of and away from disaster. It is not a rescue plan for those of us who are sinking. Our homecoming brings us to the place of peace and rest. It is the outworking of our inheritance. As we are comforted we discover our place of belonging in the Father's heart. We discover true contentment; this is part of our inheritance.

I encourage you to pursue your homecoming. It will enable you to live from a free heart and that is what I want to delve into in our final section.

Contentment

Many people are not content. They constantly seek new passions or desires, possessions or hobbies, activities or busyness. These things may not be wrong in themselves, but they are not the things that bring ultimate satisfaction or contentment. There is a constant pressure to 'have' or to 'do'. This pressure is taken away when our heart has been comforted and is content.

We've already seen the picture of contentment King David gave us in Psalm 131, but let me remind you once more.

"My heart is not proud, Lord,
my eyes are not haughty;
I do not concern myself with great matters
or things too wonderful for me.
But I have calmed and quieted myself,
I am like a weaned child with its mother;
like a weaned child I am content.
Israel, put your hope in the Lord
both now and forevermore." (Psalm 131)

Despite being the king of a large empire his heart was beautifully content in a childlike simplicity.

Being constantly comforted, even when we think we don't need to be, will cause a reservoir, or foundation, of comfort to grow in our heart. We will find life a lot easier if we are able to live out of this surplus rather than constantly trying to fill an empty hole.

Living from the overflow of comfort will cause our heart to be free. When we have a free heart we are too free to fear. We will have the confidence to try new things without fear of failure. We are more confident to be ourselves, rather than constantly trying to meet other people's expectations. In some small way we become like the twelve year old Jesus who grew in 'wisdom and in stature and in favour with God and all the people' (Luke 2:52 NLT).

As we become comfortable with who we really are then our freedom releases greater creativity. We are made in God's image and he is the Great Creator. I used to think I was not creative, at school I hated art because it was all about painting and I couldn't paint. I believed that lie for years and it was only as my heart came home that I began to believe I was, and could be, creative. Now I love photography and the creativity that is released through it. Creativity satisfies a longing within us to express who we are. We can do that more fully when we're living from a comforted heart.

A comforted heart is free of shame, guilt and condemnation and allows us to be the sons and daughters we were created to be.

We are anointed. An anointing, like so many things, is a gift. It is given by another and our Father will anoint us for the work he is giving us to do on earth. I emphasise, he anoints us to do his work. There are many good things that may need to be done, but are they the good works which have already been prepared for you or me (Ephesians 2:10)? It's all too easy to take things on, dare

I say there can even be pressure for us to take things on, but my question is always 'does it have my name on it?'

Isaiah writes of this anointing in chapter 61. He is speaking prophetically of himself. He is primarily speaking prophetically of Jesus, but he is also speaking to us.

"The Spirit of the Sovereign Lord is on me,
because the Lord has anointed me
to proclaim good news to the poor.
He has sent me to bind up the broken-hearted,
to proclaim freedom for the captives
and release from darkness for the prisoners,
to proclaim the year of the Lord's favour
and the day of vengeance of our God,
to comfort all who mourn,
and provide for those who grieve in Zion—
to bestow on them a crown of beauty instead of ashes,
the oil of joy instead of mourning,
and a garment of praise instead of a spirit of despair.
They will be called oaks of righteousness,
a planting of the Lord for the display of his splendour."
(Isaiah 61:1-4)

If we have not been comforted then there is no way we will be able do anything that is contained in this passage. We may try and it will lead us to exhaustion or feeling inadequate. We will fail and be discouraged and so try harder and harder to succeed in our own strength. We simply cannot give what we have not received.

This anointing is not for servants but is for sons and daughters. It is for those who have been comforted by the Father's love. As we are comforted we can take good news to the poor, we can bind the broken-hearted, we can set the captives free and we can proclaim the year of the Lord's favour. We will be able to comfort those who mourn with the comfort we have received.

As we live with this surplus of comfort we are awakened to the endless opportunities where God can be a Father to us.

When we view comfort as an emergency sticking plaster there remains a dissatisfaction within our heart. We are not content. Once the container of our heart is full and overflowing then the internal striving ceases and our heart finds the deep contentment and satisfaction which it truly desires.

The comfort I have been talking about is not just to set us free from past hurts. It is to set us free to live as sons and daughters, to walk as Jesus walked and to start to live and enjoy the abundant life we are promised. I end with one of my favourite verses. As we are comforted and continue to live out of the surplus of comfort we will fully understand what these words mean and we will see the fruit of them in our life.

"And I will be a Father to you, and you will be my sons and daughters,"
Says the Lord Almighty. (2 Corinthians 6:18)

Printed in Great Britain
by Amazon